I0173214

You Already Have...

All of the Tools That You Need

Special Edition

by

Lisa H. Fuller, D.O.

* * * * * * * * * * * * * *

Published by
Learn **R**ealistic **H**abits for the **F**uture

You Already Have...
All of the Tools that You Need
Special Edition

Unless otherwise indicated, all scriptures are taken from the King James Version of the Bible (KJV)

Published by
Learn **R**ealistic **H**abits for the **F**uture
This book may not be reproduced without written permission.

Cover and Interior Design by Christina Dixon

ISBN 978-09754023-0-6
Manufactured in the United States of America

I thank God
for renewed blessings and mercies
each day.

FOREWORD

No successful enterprise can be built without tools. The enterprise of life is a pursuit of purpose, impact and destiny. The operative questions are always, "Why am I here?" "What was I meant to do?" "Have I made a difference?" and "How do I fulfill my destiny?" There can be no substitute for the utilization of the proper tools to get the job done.

Dr. Lisa Fuller, noted psychiatrist and author, in this book unearths a tremendous revelation that empowers our collective consciousness. You already have the tools! We are all born on purpose with purpose. The capacity needed to fulfill those purposes lie within us. We must discover ourselves and then stir up the gift that is within us. Connect the tools inherent in you to the potential destined for you and success will be yours.

Dr. Edgar L. Vann
Senior Pastor
Second Ebenezer Church
Detroit, Michigan

There is no coincidence that you are reading this book. I pray that you will find the contents to be encouraging and uplifting in whatever circumstances that you may be facing.

Dr. Lisa H. Fuller

Acknowledge God First

In every decision, go to God first.

*I*n everything,

be careful to place God first.

But seek ye first the kingdom of God, and his righteousness; and all these things shall be added unto you.   Matthew 6:33

*I*f you go to God first,

He will provide you with instruction.

He that refuseth instruction despiseth his own soul: but he that heareth reproof getteth understanding. The fear of the Lord is the instruction of wisdom; and before honour is humility. **Proverbs 15:32-33**

"THINGS GOD HAS INSTRUCTED ME."

_____

_____

_____

_____

_____

_____

_____

_____

_____

_____

_____

_____

Change

By making a conscience effort to change your attitude, perception, and reactions, you will find that your circumstances will change.

*C*hange starts first in your mind.

And be not conformed to this world: but be ye transformed by the renewing of your mind, that ye may prove what is that good, and acceptable, and perfect, will of God.   Romans 12:2

*I*n mental imprisonment,

locks and chains are not necessary.

Fear, worry, anxiety, sadness, hopelessness,

helplessness, low self-esteem,

and poverty are the wardens and guards.

They are the deception of the enemy.

Christ holds the key to unlock

the prison cell door of your mind.

Stand fast therefore in the liberty wherewith Christ hath made us free, and be not entangled again with the yoke of bondage. Galatians 5:1

$\mathcal{H}$e provides us
with the tools that we need
to locate the key.
Utilize them.
Unlock it through prayer, fasting and hope.
Step out in faith.
Dream.
Explore and break free.
Define your limitless boundaries
not your limitations by

letting God lead your path.

Is not this the fast that I have chosen? to loose the bands of wickedness, to undo the heavy burdens, and to let the oppressed go free, and that ye break every yoke? Then shall thy light break forth as the morning, and thine health shall spring forth speedily: and thy righteousness shall go before thee; the glory of the Lord shall be thy rearward. Then shalt thou call, and the Lord shall answer; thou shalt cry, and he shall say, Here I am.
Isaiah 58:6, 8-9a

$\mathscr{Y}$ou are what and
who you believe you are.
You attract what you project.

Those who are angry create tension
and conflict within their environment.

Those who are peaceful project
calming, comforting,
Christ-minded influences.

Set your affection on things above, not on things on the earth. **Colossians 3:2**

"THINGS I WANT TO REMEMBER
AS I CHANGE."

_____

_____

_____

_____

_____

_____

_____

_____

_____

_____

_____

_____

Have Faith

&

Be Patient

Change takes time.

*B*e patient and be still.

Wait on the Lord.

But they that wait upon the Lord shall renew their strength; they shall mount up with wings as eagles; they shall run, and not be weary; and they shall walk, and not faint.   Isaiah 40:31

*B*elieve

and trust in the Lord Jesus Christ.

Through the Holy Spirit,

God will direct and guide you.

Just, let go and let God work...

on YOU

with YOU

and

through YOU.

The steps of a good man are ordered by the Lord: and he delighteth in his way.

Psalms 37:23

*S*tep out on faith.
Srive to be the best
that you can be.
Don't be disappointed
if you stumble along the way.
Let God be your pilot.
Let your faith be the fuel
that ignites and drives you.
Finishing…
Reaching your greatest potential…

takes time.

Be patient.

Now faith is the substance of things hoped for, the evidence of things not seen.
Hebrews 11:1

*H*ave you ever

prayed for something and

didn't get it when you wanted it?

Was your faith weakened?

Don't be discouraged.

God's time may not be your time.

Through prayer, fasting, faith, and hope,

You can develop the patience

to

WAIT.

Wait on the Lord: be of good courage, and he shall strengthen thine heart: wait, I say, on the Lord.

Psalms 27:14

*D*o you feel stressed out?

Overwhelmed?

Anxious?

Like giving up? Letting go?

As though there is no way out?

STOP!

Be still.

Pray.

Fast.

Meditate on God's Word.

Remember that nothing is impossible
for our Lord and Savior Jesus Christ to
Heal, Fix, Restore, Replace, or Change.
God will provide you with an escape.

Even in your darkest hour

Never Give Up!

**There hath no temptation taken you but such
as is common to man: but God is faithful, who
will not suffer you to be tempted above that ye
are able; but will with the temptation also make
a way to escape, that ye may be able to bear it.**
I Corinthians 10:13

*F*ear not.

Don't be afraid.

The **Lord Jesus Christ's** hand

is always upon you.

Through Him is your deliverance and salvation.

Jesus will destroy the ***R.O.D.S.** that satan

may cast at you.

Truly my soul waiteth upon God: from him cometh my salvation. He only is my rock and my salvation; he is my defence; I shall not be greatly moved. **Psalms 62:1-2**

"THINGS I WANT TO REMEMBER
AS I CHANGE."

_____

_____

_____

_____

_____

_____

_____

_____

_____

_____

_____

_____

Obedience Equals Prosperity

Obedience to God's Word
produces change.

*O*bedience

to God's word

produces LIFE!

If they obey and serve [him], they shall spend their days in prosperity, and their years in pleasures. But if they obey not, they shall perish by the sword, and they shall die without knowledge.   **Job 36:11-12**

$\mathcal{A}$s a result

of your obedience to God's Word,

Peace

Joy

&

Prosperity

Are yours for the taking.

Every place that the sole of your foot shall tread upon, that have I given unto you, as I said unto Moses.   Joshua 1:3

Only be thou strong and very courageous, that thou mayest observe to do according to all the law, which Moses my servant commanded thee: turn not from it to the right hand or to the left, that thou mayest prosper whithersoever thou goest.   Joshua 1:7

$\mathcal{G}$od provides you
with strength to stand upright and unbent
without swaying as you travel
through the straight gate.

Often, it is easy to sway with the breeze
instead of going against the resistance.
The swaying often turns into...

Distortion
Falsehood
and
Disparity.

Renewal and rejuvenation of your faith
can restore your travel through the straight gate.

Enter ye in at the strait gate: for wide is the gate, and broad is the way, that leadeth to destruction, and many there be which go in there at: Because strait is the gate, and narrow is the way, which leadeth unto life, and few there be that find it.

Matthew 7:13-14

"THINGS I WANT TO REMEMBER

AS I CHANGE."

_____

_____

_____

_____

_____

_____

_____

_____

_____

_____

_____

_____

God
Made You
Special

Each one of us is talented.

*T*he Lord created man

as one of His many miracles.

I am

a Miracle

and

so are

You!

In the beginning God created the heaven and the earth. **Genesis 1:1**

And God created great whales, and every living creature that moveth... **Genesis 1:21**

So God created man in his own image, in the image of God created he him... **Genesis 1:27**

$\mathcal{Y}$our life

has meaning and purpose.

Did you know that

God pre-determined

your destiny

before you were born?

Paul, an apostle of Jesus Christ by the will of God, to the saints which are at Ephesus, and to the faithful in Christ Jesus: Grace be to you, and peace, from God our Father, and from the Lord Jesus Christ. Blessed be the God and Father of our Lord Jesus Christ, who hath blessed us with all spiritual blessings in heavenly places in Christ: According as he hath chosen us in him before the foundation of the world, that we should be holy and without blame before him in love: Having predestinated us unto the adoption of children by Jesus Christ to himself, according to the good pleasure of his will, To the praise of the glory of his grace, wherein he hath made us accepted in the beloved.

Ephesians 1:1-6

In whom we have redemption through his blood, the forgiveness of sins, according to the riches of his grace; Wherein he hath abounded toward us in all wisdom and prudence; Having made known unto us the mystery of his will, according to his good pleasure which he hath purposed in himself: That in the dispensation of the fulness of times he might gather together in one all things in Christ, both which are in heaven, and which are on earth; even in him:

Ephesians 1:7-10

In whom also we have obtained an inheritance, being predestinated according to the purpose of him who worketh all things after the counsel of his own will: That we should be to the praise of his glory, who first trusted in Christ. In whom ye also trusted, after that ye heard the word of truth, the gospel of your salvation: in whom also after that ye believed, ye were sealed with that holy Spirit of promise, Which is the earnest of our inheritance until the redemption of the purchased possession, unto the praise of his glory.

Ephesians 1:11-14

Wherefore I also, after I heard of your faith in the Lord Jesus, and love unto all the saints, Cease not to give thanks for you, making mention of you in my prayers;

Ephesians 1:15-16

$\mathcal{G}$od gave

each one of us unique talents and gifts.

You are special.

Now there are diversities of gifts, but the same Spirit. And there are differences of administrations, but the same Lord. And there are diversities of operations, but it is the same God which worketh all in all. But the manifestation of the Spirit is given to every man to profit withal. For to one is given by the Spirit the word of wisdom; to another the word of knowledge by the same Spirit;

To another faith by the same Spirit; to another gifts of healing by the same Spirit;

To another the working of miracles; to another prophecy; to another discerning of spirits; to another [divers] kinds of tongues; to another the interpretation of tongues: But all these worketh that one and the selfsame Spirit, dividing to every man severally as he will.

I Corinthians 12:4-11

*U*se your talents.

Don't waste them!

For the kingdom of heaven is as a man travelling into a far country, who called his own servants, and delivered unto them his goods. And unto one he gave five talents, to another two, and to another one; to every man according to his several ability; and straightway took his journey. Then he that had received the five talents went and traded with the same, and made them other five talents. And likewise he that had received two, he also gained other two. But he that had received one went and digged in the earth, and hid his lord's money.

Matthew 25:14-18

And so he that had received five talents came and brought other five talents, saying, Lord, thou deliveredst unto me five talents: behold, I have gained beside them five talents more. His lord said unto him, Well done, thou good and faithful servant: thou hast been faithful over a few things, I will make thee ruler over many things: enter thou into the joy of thy lord.

Matthew 25:20-21

He also that had received two talents came and said, Lord, thou deliveredst unto me two talents: behold, I have gained two other talents beside them. His lord said unto him, Well done, good and faithful servant; thou hast been faithful over a few things, I will make thee ruler over many things: enter thou into the joy of thy lord.

Matthew 25:22-23

Then he which had received the one talent came and said, Lord, I knew thee that thou art an hard man, reaping where thou hast not sown, and gathering where thou hast not strawed: And I was afraid, and went and hid thy talent in the earth: lo, there thou hast that is thine. His lord answered and said unto him, Thou wicked and slothful servant, thou knewest that I reap where I sowed not, and gather where I have not strawed: Thou oughtest therefore to have put my money to the exchangers, and then at my coming I should have received mine own with usury. Take therefore the talent from him, and give it unto him which hath ten talents. For unto every one that hath shall be given, and he shall have abundance: but from him that hath not shall be taken away even that which he hath.

Mathew 25:24-29

"THINGS I WANT TO REMEMBER AS I CHANGE."

_____

_____

_____

_____

_____

_____

_____

_____

_____

_____

_____

Reflection

*R*egardless of the circumstances, the decision to make change first starts in the mind. Indecisiveness, depression, jealousy, insecurity, addiction, anger, lust, and debt are examples of circumstances that can be changed by changing ones mindset regardless of the situation. As we include God first in every aspect of our lives, make a commitment to change, have faith, and patience, we will begin to see our circumstances change.

...all the days of appointed time will I wait, till my change come.   Job 14:14b

"THINGS I WANT TO REMEMBER

AS I CHANGE."

_____

_____

_____

_____

_____

_____

_____

_____

_____

_____

_____

_____

"THINGS I WANT TO REMEMBER AS I CHANGE."

_____

_____

_____

_____

_____

_____

_____

_____

_____

_____

_____

_____

If you want to accept Jesus Christ into your life as Lord and Savior, you can do so by praying the following prayer.

God, I repent of my sins. From this day forth, I accept Jesus Christ into my life to become Lord over it. I believe that Jesus Christ is the Son of God, died on the cross to pay the price for my sins, and rose from the grave on the third day ascending to Heaven. By accepting Jesus Christ into my life, I have received the gift of eternal life.

Amen.

If you just prayed the previous prayer, the following scriptures provide confirmation of what you just did.

*   **That if thou shalt confess with thy mouth the Lord Jesus, and shalt believe in thine heart that God hath raised him from the dead, thou shalt be saved.   Romans 10:9**

*   **Whosoever shall confess that Jesus is the Son of God, God dwelleth in him and he in God.   I John 4:15**

*   **Verily, verily, I say unto you, He that believeth on me hath everlasting life.**
    John 6:47

*   **Behold, I stand at the door, and knock: if any man hear my voice, and open the door, I will come in to him, and will sup with him, and he with me.   Revelation 3:20**

*   **Verily, verily, I say unto you, He that heareth my word, and believeth on him that sent me, hath everlasting life, and shall not come into condemnation; but is passed from death unto life.   John 5:24**

ABOUT THE AUTHOR:

Dr. Lisa H. Fuller

"Until I surrendered to God and the calling that He placed on me, my life was unbalanced. It was not until I experienced brokenness and accepted Christ that I came to the awareness of God's love and the understanding of God's purpose for my life. At that point, I realized that God had already put inside me *ALL of the TOOLS THAT I NEED*."

Products by Dr. Lisa H. Fuller

You Already Have... All of the Tools that You Need
(Book) - Are you tired of feeling sad, depressed, angry, hopeless, being in debt, or having an addiction? God has given you all of the tools that you need to change. Change first starts in your mind.

God is Love
(Book) When you find yourself feeling like no one cares don't forget that God is love.

To Purchase products visit:
www.LisaHFullerMinistries.org

Contact Dr. Lisa

Dr. Fuller is available for book signings, presentations, lectures, and media appearances. For more information or send all inquiries to:

Website: LisaHFullerMinistries.org

Email: LisaHFullerMinistries@gmail.com

Facebook: LisaHFullerMinistries

Phone: (313) 398-3131

www.ingramcontent.com/pod-product-compliance
Lightning Source LLC
Chambersburg PA
CBHW060409050426
42449CB00009B/1939